BRIGHT
IDEA
BOOKS

HOW DO Robots DEFUSE BOMBS?

by Yvette LaPierre

Content Consultant
Aviral Shrivastava
Associate Professor
School of Computing Informatics and
Decision Systems Engineering
Arizona State University

CAPSTONE PRESS
a capstone imprint

Bright Idea Books are published by Capstone Press
1710 Roe Crest Drive, North Mankato, Minnesota 56003
www.mycapstone.com

Library of Congress Cataloging-in-Publication Data
Names: LaPierre, Yvette, 1963- author.
Title: How do robots diffuse bombs? / by Yvette LaPierre.
Description: North Mankato, Minnesota : Capstone Press, [2019] | Series:
   How'd they do that? | Audience: Grades 4 to 6. | Includes bibliographical
   references and index.
Identifiers: LCCN 2018018715 (print) | LCCN 2018019868 (ebook) | ISBN
   9781543541793 (ebook) | ISBN 9781543541397 (hardcover : alk. paper)
Subjects: LCSH: Robots--Juvenile literature. | Military robots--Juvenile
   literature. | Explosive ordnance disposal--Safety measures--Automatic
   control--Juvenile literature. | Police--Special weapons and tactics
   units--Equipment and supplies--Juvenile literature.
Classification: LCC TP270.5 (ebook) | LCC TP270.5 .L37 2019 (print) | DDC
   629.8/92--dc23
LC record available at https://lccn.loc.gov/2018018715

Editorial Credits
Editor: Megan Gunderson
Designer: Becky Daum
Production Specialist: Colleen McLaren

Photo Credits
Alamy: Alain Le Garsmeur "The Troubles" Archive, 17, Open Government License, 18–19, 20; AP Images: Matthias Balk/picture-alliance/dpa, 8–9, 28, Press Association/URN:8519730, 23, Wally Santana, 11; iStockphoto: Caluian, 30–31; Shutterstock Images: ChameleonsEye, 5, Quality Stock Arts, 12–13; US Air Force: Staff Sgt. Manuel J. Martinez, 24–25; US Navy: Mass Communication Specialist 1st Class Peter D. Lawlor, cover, Mass Communication Specialist 2nd Class Derek R. Sanchez, 14–15, Mass Communication Specialist 3rd Class Jumar T. Balacy, 27, Mass Communication Specialist Seaman Charles Oki, 6–7

Design Elements: iStockphoto, Red Line Editorial, and Shutterstock Images

Special thanks to Lekha Shrivastava for her feedback on this book.

TABLE OF CONTENTS

CHAPTER 1

A ROBOT SAVES
the Day

A soldier is on patrol. He sees a package. It is hidden under a car. It could be a bomb. But it is dangerous to get too close.

Soldiers watch out for danger.

The robot rolls on treads like a small tank.

Another soldier stands at a safe distance. She sends in a **remote-controlled** robot.

The robot moves toward the car. It has a camera. This helps the soldier see from far away.

A robot uses special tools to take apart bombs.

The robot has an arm. The arm has tools on it. The arm reaches out. The tools cut wires. The bomb has been **defused**. The street is safe!

CHAPTER 2

MILITARY
Robots

Robots are machines. Computers control their movements. People write the instructions for the computers.

A soldier uses a controller. He sends a robot into dangerous places.

iRobot makes robots that defuse bombs. It also makes Roomba, the robot vacuum.

ROBOTS AT WORK

Robots do many jobs. Some explore other planets. Some work in factories. Others clean homes.

The military uses robots. Robots collect information. They spy. They do dangerous jobs. They keep military members safe.

THE FIRST ROBOTS

The word *robot* was first used in 1921 in a play. It comes from a word meaning "forced labor."

Special suits help protect soldiers from bombs. Using robots is safer.

ROBOTS VS. BOMBS

One dangerous job is bomb **disposal**. There are two ways to dispose of a bomb. It can be towed to a safe place and exploded. Or it can be defused.

Soldiers did this job for many years. Many lost their lives. The military wanted bomb disposal to be safer. Robots were perfect for the job.

CHAPTER 3

THE
Wheelbarrow

The first bomb disposal robot was the Wheelbarrow. It was made in 1972. It was an electric wheelbarrow. It had a hook on the front. It could hook a bomb and tow it to safety. But the Wheelbarrow had problems.

A soldier controlled the Wheelbarrow with long ropes. The robot could only go the length of the ropes. Sometimes the ropes got tangled.

Robot makers needed to improve the Wheelbarrow.

Engineers found a solution. They added computers. Now soldiers control the robots without ropes or wires. They use **joysticks**, like a computer game.

A modern Wheelbarrow can destroy suspected bombs.

MORE PROBLEMS SOLVED

The soldier could now stand far away. But he needed to see the bomb. Engineers put cameras on the robot. The soldier watches through a monitor. He can see what the robot is doing.

A Wheelbarrow's arm can remove a bomb from under a car.

Early robots had trouble on uneven ground. They tipped over. Engineers replaced the wheels with treads. Treads roll over rocky ground. They even climb stairs.

The Wheelbarrow could tow a bomb away. It could not defuse a bomb. Then engineers added an arm. It had a hand. Its joints moved. The hand had tools to take apart bombs.

POLICE ROBOTS

Police also use robots to dispose of bombs.

CHAPTER 4

BOMB DISPOSAL
Robots
Today

Today's robots carry many tools. They can go almost anywhere. They come in many sizes.

A soldier can carry the
Dragon Runner robot
in a backpack.

Soldiers practice controlling a PackBot.

SMALL BOTS

Soldiers find bombs in tight places.

The iRobot company made the PackBot.

The PackBot can fit in a backpack.
Soldiers can roll it under cars. They
throw it through windows. It can turn
itself over if it lands on its back.

ROBOT SUPERPOWERS

Some robots use X-ray vision to
find bombs.

BIG BOTS

Some bomb disposal robots are big. They are the size of bulldozers! They roll on treads. They have a big arm. They clear large fields of **mines** and bombs.

SEA BOTS

Sometimes bombs are underwater. Some robots work in shallow water. The navy uses robot subs. They hunt for mines in the ocean.

Robots go into dangerous places. They get rid of bombs safely. These robots are saving lives.

The U.S. Navy uses robots to clear underwater bombs.

GLOSSARY

defuse
to take apart a bomb before it explodes

disposal
the act of getting rid of or turning into trash

engineer
a person who designs machines or structures

joystick
a control stick

mine
an explosive device

remote-controlled
operated from a distance

TRIVIA

1. Soldiers use the Talon robot to search for bombs.
    Police officers use this robot too. It can have up
    to seven cameras. One camera is for night vision.

2. The U.S. Navy trains dolphins and sea lions to look
    for mines in the ocean. Robots may soon replace
    the animals.

3. The military uses robots that fly too. These robots
    spy on enemies from the air. They are called
    drones.

4. In the future, robots might work in teams. One can
    find the bomb. The other can defuse it.

YouTube has lots of videos of bomb-defusing robots at work. Ask an adult to help you find a robot video. It should feature a robot that is not in this book, such as Robo Sally or RE2. Watch a mission from start to finish. Then write your own description of the robot. How is it similar to robots in this book? How is it different?

Military robots can do lots of things. But they aren't perfect. What improvements would you make? What else could robots do for soldiers?

FURTHER RESOURCES

Learn more about robot science:

Faust, Daniel R., *Building Robots: Robotic Engineers.*
  New York: PowerKids Press, 2016.

Robotics Facts from Idaho Public Television
http://idahoptv.org/sciencetrek/topics/robots/facts.cfm

Robots on Explain That Stuff!
http://www.explainthatstuff.com/robots.html

Check out robots the military uses on important missions:

Alpert, Barbara. *U.S. Military Robots*. North Mankato, MN: Capstone Press, 2013.

Five Bomb Disposal Robots
https://www.roboticstomorrow.com/article/2015/10/five-bomb-disposal-
  robots/6987/

White, Steve. *Military Robots*. New York: Children's Press, 2007.

INDEX